# BRUGES TRAVEL GUIDE 2023

**Explore Bruges: Ultimate guide to top attraction, accommodation, when to visit and how to get around Bruges**

**Diana H. Cayer**

# TABLE OF CONTENT

# INTRODUCTION

The lovely medieval city of Bruges in Belgium is a must-see for all tourists. Bruges provides a distinctive fusion of history, culture, and contemporary conveniences with its scenic canals, cobblestone streets, and stunning buildings. A wonderfully enchanting destination, it is a city that has preserved its medieval history while embracing the present.

Bruges has a lengthy history that reaches back to the ninth century and is the capital of West Flanders. Bruges, which previously served as a significant hub for the trade of lace and textiles, earned the nickname "Venice of the North" for its extensive system of canals. Today, Bruges is a well-known tourist destination that draws millions of visitors each year and is designated as a UNESCO World Heritage Site.

We try to give you all the details you need to organize your trip to this wonderful city in this Bruges travel guide. We will go through everything you need to know to make sure your vacation to Bruges is enjoyable and memorable, from getting there and choosing lodging to touring the historic district and trying the local food.

Bruges offers something for everyone, regardless of your interests in art, architecture, history, or simply soaking up the atmosphere of a quaint European city. There are many activities to keep you engaged, such as wandering along the canals and tasting some of the best chocolate and beer in the world.

We therefore encourage you to go with us to Bruges, where the past and present meet together in a truly spectacular way, whether you are planning a romantic trip or a family vacation.

## Overview of Bruges

The picturesque historic city of Bruges, also known as Brugge in Dutch, is situated in the northwest of Belgium. The city, which serves as the provincial capital of West Flanders, is located about 100 kilometers northwest of Brussels. Bruges is referred described as the "Venice of the North" because of its beautiful architecture, cobblestone streets, and lovely canals.

The Vikings established Bruges as a tiny harbor town in the ninth century, beginning the city's history. During the

Middle Ages, it quickly expanded in size and significance and turned into a significant hub for trade and commerce. The city served as a center for the textile industry as well as the production of lace and other high-end goods due to its location at the confluence of several significant trade routes.

Bruges was one of the richest and most significant cities in Europe in the 14th and 15th centuries, rivaling cities like Venice, Florence, and London. Some of the city's most recognizable structures, such as the Belfry, the Church of Our Lady, and the Basilica of the Holy Blood, were built as a result of its advantageous location and burgeoning economy.

However, as the port of Antwerp became more significant and Bruges lost its strategic advantage, the city's fortunes started to decline in the 16th century. Until the 19th century, when a number of Belgian intellectuals and artists started to show interest in the city's rich history and cultural legacy, the city went into a period of decline and was mostly forgotten.

Today, Bruges is a well-known tourist destination that draws millions of visitors each year and is designated as a UNESCO World Heritage Site. The city's antique structures, canals, and winding lanes have all managed to retain much of their original charm and character from the Middle Ages.

The historic core of Bruges, which is home to some of the city's most recognizable landmarks, such as the Belfry, the Church of Our Lady, and the Beguinage, is one of the city's most well-liked attractions. The Church of Our Lady is a magnificent Gothic church that includes several significant works of art, including a marble sculpture by Michelangelo. The Belfry is a medieval bell tower that provides breathtaking views of the city from its summit.

Bruges is renowned for its outstanding gastronomy and regional delicacies, such as Belgian chocolate, waffles, and beer, in addition to its historical sites. These delicacies are available for sampling at any of the numerous eateries and cafes spread around the city.

In general, Bruges is a city that provides a special fusion of heritage, culture, and contemporary amenities. For everyone interested in learning more about Europe's rich cultural legacy, it is a must-visit location since it is a site where the past and present meld together in a truly magical way.

## History of Bruges

When the Vikings established Bruges as a little port town in the ninth century, it began a long and fascinating history. The city expanded in size and significance over the years, becoming a significant hub for trade and commerce in the Middle Ages.

Bruges was one of the richest and most significant cities in Europe throughout the 14th and 15th centuries, rivaling cities like Venice, Florence, and London. Due to its advantageous location at the confluence of several significant trade routes, it served as a center for the production of lace and other upscale items in addition to textiles.

Some of Bruges' most recognizable structures, such as the Belfry, the Church of Our Lady, and the Basilica of the Holy Blood, were built as a result of this prosperity. The Church of Our Lady, a magnificent Gothic church that includes several significant works of art, including a marble sculpture by Michelangelo, was constructed in the 15th century, while the Belfry, a medieval bell tower that affords breathtaking views of the city from its top, was finished in the 14th century.

However, as Antwerp's port gained importance and Bruges lost its strategic advantage, Bruges' fortunes started to decline in the 16th century. Until the 19th century, when a number of Belgian intellectuals and artists started to show interest in the city's rich history and cultural legacy, the city went into a period of decline and was mostly forgotten.

Today, Bruges is a well-known tourist destination that draws millions of visitors each year and is designated as a

UNESCO World Heritage Site. The city's antique structures, canals, and winding lanes have all managed to retain much of their original charm and character from the Middle Ages. For everyone interested in learning more about Europe's rich cultural legacy, this city is a must-visit. It offers a distinctive fusion of history, culture, and contemporary conveniences.

## Geography and the climate

The city of Bruges, which is in northwest Belgium, experiences warm maritime winters and chilly summers. The city has a temperate climate with regular rains throughout the year, which is impacted by its closeness to the North Sea.

Geographically speaking, Bruges is located on Belgium's western coast and is encircled by a system of canals and waterways. The city is situated on the flat Flanders plains, about 15 kilometers inland from the North Sea.

Polders, low-lying portions of land that have been reclaimed from the sea and are guarded by dikes and levees, are a prominent feature of the area surrounding Bruges. These polders have been utilized for agriculture for many years; popular products grown there include potatoes, sugar beets, and chicory.

The city of Bruges is constructed on a number of little islands that are linked by a system of canals and bridges. With its flowing canals, medieval structures, and tiny alleyways, the city's historic core is especially attractive.

Although Bruges' canals are still used for tourism, they were once used for trade and transportation. Boat excursions of the city's canals are available to visitors, and they provide a distinctive perspective on the city's architecture and history.

The area surrounding Bruges is distinguished by a variety of grasslands, wetlands, and woodlands in terms of vegetation and wildlife. Particularly significant for birdlife are the wetlands that surround the city, which are home to species like the grey heron, Eurasian coot, and common pochard.

Overall, Bruges' terrain and climate have a significant impact on the way the city is characterized and who it is. The city's growth has been significantly aided by its location near the North Sea and the availability of canals and waterways, while the surrounding area's fertile soil and temperate temperature have supported a thriving agricultural sector. Bruges continues to be a distinctive and beautiful city that draws tourists from all over the world.

## Why Travel to Bruges?

Whether you're interested in history, art, food, or just taking in the magnificent surroundings, Bruges is a city that has something for everyone. Here are just a few reasons to think about going to Bruges:

Historic architecture: Some of Europe's most stunning and well-preserved historic buildings may be found in Bruges.

The Gothic Church of Our Lady, the Belfry, and the Basilica of the Holy Blood are just a few of the spectacular structures that can be seen in the city's medieval center, which is a UNESCO World Heritage Site. The city's winding, cobblestone streets transport you back in time as you stroll through them.

Art & culture: Bruges is also the site of many noteworthy artistic and cultural landmarks. The Memling Museum is devoted to the works of Hans Memling, a Flemish painter from the 15th century, while the Groeningemuseum displays an extraordinary collection of Flemish and Belgian art. The city also has a vibrant cultural environment, with year-round performances, festivals, and other events.

Food and drink: Beer and chocolate are two of Belgium's most well-known exports, and Bruges is no exception. Numerous breweries can be found in the city, including the De Halve Maan brewery, which makes the well-known Brugse Zot beer. The city is also home to many chocolate stores that sell a variety of delectable sweets.

Canals and waterways: Due to its extensive network of canals and waterways, Bruges is frequently referred to as the "Venice of the North." A wonderful opportunity to explore the city from a different angle and appreciate the magnificent architecture and surroundings is to take a boat trip of the city's canals.

Last but not least, Bruges is a fantastic spot to unwind and unwind. The city's relaxed atmosphere, attractive streets, and quaint cafes and restaurants make it the ideal location for relaxation and energy restoration.

Overall, there is something for everyone in Bruges. You may find something to enjoy in this lovely and attractive city whether you're into history, art, food, or just relaxing.

# CHAPTER 1

## Travel Planning to Bruges

An exciting and satisfying experience can be had when organizing a trip to Bruges, Belgium. Bruges is a place that is likely to enchant tourists of all ages and interests with its fascinating history, beautiful architecture, delectable cuisine, and picturesque canals. To make the most of your trip, you should spend the necessary time to plan and prepare before you leave on your adventure.

Everything you need to know to organize your trip to Bruges will be provided in this book, including advice on when to travel, where to stay, what to see and do, and how to navigate the city.

This book will assist you in planning a pleasant and pleasurable journey to this lovely city, whether you're visiting alone, with friends, family, or on a romantic break.

Therefore, let's get going and start making plans for your ideal trip to Bruges!

## Best time to visit Bruges

Even though Bruges is a lovely city to visit all year round, the ideal time to go depends on your preferences and considerations. When making travel plans, it's important to take into account variables like weather, crowds, and activities because each season in Bruges offers a distinctive experience.

### (March – May) spring

As the weather starts to warm up and the city fills with flowers and greenery, spring is a lovely time to visit Bruges. Minnewater Park's well-known daffodils and tulips begin to bloom, providing a lovely setting for a stroll or picnic. If you're interested in cultural events and festivals, like the Holy Blood Procession in May, this is also an excellent time to visit Bruges.

(June through August)

Due to the warm, sunny weather and the fact that the city is in full swing, the summer is the busiest and most favored season to visit Bruges. The drawback of this time of year is that queues for famous sights like the Belfry can be extremely long and the crowds can be overwhelming.

However, summer is also a great time to engage in outdoor pursuits like picnics in parks or canal boat tours. The Bruges Summer Festival, which takes place in July, is only one of several festivals and activities that take place all summer long.

(September to November)

Bruges is a lovely place to visit in the fall when the leaves are changing and the city has an inviting, autumnal atmosphere. The crowds are dwindling as the summer season draws to a close, and the weather is moderate and agreeable. Fall is also a fantastic time to try some of the delectable seasonal fare and libations that Bruges is known for, including waffles, beer, and chocolate.

(December to February) Winter

As the city is transformed into a winter wonderland with festive decorations, ice skating rinks, and Christmas markets, winter is a magical time to visit Bruges. Even though it may be chilly and rainy outside, the festive mood and inviting ambiance more than make up for it. A must-see site, the Bruges Christmas Market has stalls selling holiday snacks, handcrafted items, and festive accents.

Overall, your unique preferences and interests will determine the best time to visit Bruges. Summer is a terrific season to travel if you want pleasant weather and lots of outdoor activities. Fall and spring are excellent choices if you like less crowded areas and colder temps.

Winter is the ideal time to travel if you want to experience the beauty of the Christmas season. Bruges is a city that will enchant and delight you with its beauty, charm, and history no matter when you visit.

# Getting to Bruges

Bruges is a well-liked vacation spot and is conveniently reachable from many significant European towns. Whether you're traveling to Bruges from within Belgium or from a distance, there are a number of transportation alternatives to take into account.

## By Air

The airport in Brussels, which is around 100 kilometers from Bruges, is the closest one. You may travel directly to Bruges from Brussels Airport by rail, which takes about one hour and fifteen minutes. Alternately, you can fly into other close-by airports like Ostend-Bruges International Airport or Lille Airport, both of which are about an hour away by train or car.

## By train

Two train stations in Bruges—Bruges-Saint-Peters and Brugge—have good connections to other significant European cities. There are direct trains that leave from Brussels and take about one hour and fifteen minutes. With a change in Brussels, the trip from Paris takes about 3 hours and 30 minutes. You can take the Eurostar from London to Brussels and then change to a direct train to Bruges.

## By Car

The city center of Bruges is a pedestrianized area, so if you're arriving by automobile, it's necessary to be aware of this. The Brugge Station parking lot and the Biekorf parking garage are only a couple of the parking alternatives available outside of the city. Driving to Bruges from adjacent cities like Brussels or Ghent is another option.

By Bus

Numerous bus companies provide services from nearby cities like Brussels, Ghent, and Antwerp to Bruges. Depending on the route and traffic, the travel duration can vary, but it often lasts between one and two hours.

## By Bike

Another alternative for the more daring traveler is to bike to Bruges. The North Sea Cycle Route and the Flanders Cycle Route are only two of the cycling routes that are easily accessible from the city. The city center has bike rentals accessible, and many hotels also provide these services.

Regardless of your mode of transportation, it's crucial to prepare in advance and take convenience, cost, and time of journey into account. Getting to Bruges is a crucial step in planning a successful trip, whether you prefer the ease of flying or the gorgeous path of cycling.

## Visa requirement

Prior to traveling, it's crucial to be aware of the visa requirements if you're thinking about visiting Bruges. Depending on your nationality, the reason for your travel, and the length of your stay, you may need a visa or not.

You do not require a visa to visit Bruges if you are a citizen of the European Union (EU) or the European Economic Area (EEA). Without a visa, you are permitted to enter and stay in Belgium for up to 90 days. However, you must have a current passport or national ID card on you at all times.

You could require a visa to enter Bruges if you're a citizen of a nation that isn't an EU or EEA member. The kind of visa you need depends on why you're visiting. You must apply for a Schengen visa if you intend to go there for pleasure or business. With a Schengen visa, you are able to freely move among the 26 European nations that make up the Schengen region, including Belgium.

You must submit an application to the Belgian embassy or consulate in your native country in order to obtain a Schengen visa. Your personal information, travel schedule, and financial details, including bank statements and evidence of travel insurance, are typically required as part of the application process.

It is crucial to remember that applying for a visa might take several weeks, therefore it is recommended to do so well in advance of your intended trip. A Schengen visa's price can also change based on how long you want to stay and what kind of visa you need.

Other visa categories, such as student, work, or family reunification visas, may be necessary in addition to the Schengen visa for particular circumstances. It is advised to check with the Belgian embassy or consulate in your home country if you are unsure whether you need a visa for your trip to Bruges.

Your country, the reason for your trip, and the length of your stay will all affect whether you need a visa to enter Bruges. If you are an EU or EEA national, you do not require a visa; however, if you are a citizen of a non-EU or non-EEA nation, you may need to apply for a Schengen visa. To ensure a simple and hassle-free vacation, it is crucial to prepare ahead of time and apply for the necessary visa well before your departure.

## Currency and money

It's crucial to have a solid understanding of the local currency and banking system before organizing a trip to Bruges. This detailed guide to Bruges's money and currency is provided.

# Currency

The euro is the official currency of Bruges. While some establishments in tourist areas might accept other currencies, like US dollars or British pounds, it's important to keep in mind that exchange rates might not be in your favor. When visiting Bruges, it is best to have cash in euros.

## ATMs:

Bruges has many ATMs, especially in the popular tourist locations. Visa, Mastercard, and Maestro are just a few of the widely accepted credit and debit cards. When using ATMs abroad, it's crucial to inquire with your bank about any possible fees or foreign transaction charges.

## Banks:

ING, KBC, BNP Paribas Fortis, and Argenta are just a few of the banks in Bruges. Belgian banks typically open from 9 am to 4 pm on weekdays, while some might stay open later on Thursdays or Fridays.

**Charge cards:**

In Bruges, credit cards are accepted almost everywhere, especially in bigger facilities like hotels, restaurants, and shops. The two credit cards that are most frequently accepted in Belgium are Visa and Mastercard. The fact that some smaller shops might only accept cash makes it vital to keep some Euros on hand.

**Tipping:**

In Bruges, tips are not required but are always appreciated. In restaurants, it's typical to round up to the nearest Euro or leave a modest tip as a show of gratitude for the helpful staff. Although it is not customary for taxi drivers to accept tips, it is considered polite to round up to the nearest Euro.

## Rates of exchange

Various variables can cause changes in the Euro's exchange rate with other currencies. To obtain an idea of how much your money is worth before going to Bruges, it's crucial to verify the exchange rate at the time. It's a good idea to investigate if your bank or credit card provider offers competitive conversion rates as well.

Modern and well-connected, Bruges offers a wide variety of banking and currency exchange services. When visiting Bruges, it's crucial to have euros on hand, and you should be aware of any fees or foreign transaction charges that might be incurred when using an ATM or a credit card. You can guarantee a simple and trouble-free experience with money and currency in Bruges by being well-informed and organized.

## What to bring

It's crucial to prepare the appropriate goods for a vacation to Bruges in order to guarantee a comfortable and happy experience. Here is a detailed packing list for your trip to Bruges.

> ➤ A pair of relaxed walking shoes

Bruges is a lovely city to see on foot, with lots of historical structures, museums, and marketplaces to see. The city's canals and cobblestone streets must be explored in good walking shoes.

> ➢ **Proper attire for the climate**

It's crucial to carry layers of clothing because Bruges's weather may be erratic. Lightweight clothes is appropriate in the summer, but it's always a good idea to pack a light jacket or sweater for chilly evenings. Warm apparel, including a coat, hat, gloves, and scarf, is necessary in the winter.

> ➢ **A cloche or raincoat**

Because Bruges frequently experiences rain, it's crucial to have a dependable umbrella or rain jacket on hand. A excellent alternative is a little umbrella that fits easily into a bag or backpack.

> ➢ **Adaptor**

In contrast to the majority of other nations, Belgium uses type E power outlets. Bring a universal adaptor so you can charge all of your devices.

➤ **Camera**

Bruges is a beautiful city with lots of places to take pictures. For recollections of your vacation, make sure to have a camera or smartphone with a good camera.

➤ **Daypack vs. backpack**

When exploring the city, a backpack or daypack is an easy way to transport necessities like water, snacks, and a map.

➤ **Guidebook**

A guidebook is a practical tool for exploring a new city and learning about its landmarks and history. Lonely Planet and Rick Steves are two excellent Bruges travel guides that are available.

➤ **Toiletries**

Remember to take necessities like your toothbrush, toothpaste, and other toiletries. It's a good idea to pack your own toiletries even if the majority of hotels offer the bare minimum.

➤ **Travel papers**

Keep all of your trip-related documents, such as your passport, travel insurance, and tickets, in a safe and secure location.

It's important to carefully consider the weather, activities, and cultural customs while making a packing list for a vacation to Bruges. You may guarantee a pleasant and happy stay in this lovely city by packing the appropriate essentials. Before you leave, be sure to check the weather forecast and pack appropriately. You can fully experience everything that Bruges has to offer with the appropriate planning.

#

# CHAPTER 2

## Getting Around Bruges

D ue to its small size and well-connected transportation system, Bruges is a reasonably simple city to navigate. In order to see the city's numerous attractions, Bruges offers a variety of forms of transportation. There are various options to select from, including public transportation, cycling, walking, and private taxis.

We'll go through the various modes of transportation in Bruges in this guide to help you organize your trip and move around the city with ease. There is a mode of transportation available for every kind of traveler, whether they want to take a tour of the old city or head out into the countryside.

## Using Public Transit

Whether you're a local or just visiting, taking the public transportation is a great way to move around Bruges. The city has a dependable and reasonably priced bus network that connects to different areas of the city and its suburbs. Here is a detailed guide to using public transportation in Bruges.

## Bus

In Bruges, the bus is the most widely used kind of public transit. The neighborhood's bus operator, known as "De Lijn," runs a wide-ranging network of buses throughout the city and its environs. The air-conditioned, air-conditioned, and modern buses are a great way to navigate around Bruges, especially in the hot months.

The majority of the city's top tourist destinations, including the old city center, museums, and the suburbs, are serviced by the bus routes. The cost of the bus is determined by the distance, and tickets can be bought from the bus driver or from ticket machines at bus stops. A variety of tickets, including single rides, day passes, and multi-day passes, are offered.

## Tram

Additionally, a tram network links Bruges to the nearby city of Blankenberge. The tram, which runs along the coast and provides breathtaking views of the North Sea, is a beautiful way to get between the two cities. Throughout the year, the tram runs every ten minutes during the busiest times.

## Train

Bruges Central and Bruges-Saint-Peter are Bruges' two train stations. Both stations provide connections to important Belgian cities as well as nearby nations like the Netherlands and France. If you want to visit surrounding cities for the day, the train is a convenient method to get to and from Bruges.

## Bicycle

In Bruges, cycling is a common means of transportation, and the city provides visitors with a variety of rental alternatives. The various parks and green areas of the city are perfect for exploring on bicycles, and many of the city's attractions are close by. Bruges offers a number of bike paths and lanes specifically for cyclists, making commuting around the city safe and pleasurable.

Bruges' public transit system provides a convenient and economical means of transportation. The extensive bus and tram network in the city makes it simple to reach the main attractions, while the rail network offers connections to neighboring cities. Cycling is another well-liked choice, and tourists may easily rent bikes. Visitors can easily and conveniently tour the city and its surroundings by taking public transit.

## Walking

The best method to travel around Bruges is probably on foot. Since the city is small, most of the top attractions are close to one another. Walking also enables visitors to take in the charm and beauty of the city up close as they wander along the cobblestone streets and ancient structures.

The following are some advantages of exploring Bruges by foot:

Cost-effective: Since walking is free, it is a great choice for tourists on a tight budget who wish to reduce their transportation expenses.

Walking is a low-impact workout that is good for people of all ages and fitness levels. It is a great way to stay active while on vacation, burn calories, and strengthen your cardiovascular system.

Route with scenic views: Walking enables tourists to take in the splendor of the city's historic buildings, parks, and canals.

Flexibility: Travelers can freely explore a city on foot at their own pace and on their own timetable. They are free to pause at any time to take pictures, dine, or shop.

Benefits for the environment: Walking is an environmentally beneficial method to get around Bruges. It is a sustainable mode of transportation because it does not cause noise or air pollution.

Even though walking is a practical way to get around Bruges, it's important to wear comfortable shoes, especially if you intend to walk for an extended period of time. To avoid getting lost, visitors should also bring a map or utilize a navigation program on their phone.

An excellent way to navigate Bruges is by foot. It is economical, healthy, adaptable, and environmentally friendly. Visitors can explore the city's numerous attractions, enjoy the picturesque surroundings, and get a personal sense of Bruges' allure and beauty.

## Biking

Another well-liked method of getting around Bruges is by bike. The city is renowned for its extensive network of bike routes and infrastructure that supports bicycle use, making it simple for tourists to explore the city on two wheels.

The following are some advantages of riding through Bruges:

Effective: Because biking is faster than walking, tourists may see more of the city in less time and cover more ground. Biking is a sustainable means of transportation that does not add to noise or air pollution, making it a great option for those who care about the environment.

Cost-effective: Renting a bike is relatively inexpensive when compared to other forms of transportation, making it a cheap way to travel around Bruges.

Fun and enjoyable: Travelers may see Bruges in a distinctive and unforgettable way by biking throughout the city.

Health advantages: Travelers can keep active and healthy while on vacation by biking, a low-impact form of exercise. Additionally, it is a fantastic way to increase cardiovascular health and burn calories.

In Bruges, there are lots of places to hire bikes, and they come in all different shapes and sizes, including tandem cycles, electric bikes, and conventional bikes. Depending on their needs, visitors can rent bikes for a few hours or for the entire day.

Visitors should wear a helmet and carry a map or use a navigation app on their phone before using the bike routes to prevent getting lost. Additionally, it's crucial to follow traffic regulations and ride cautiously, especially on congested streets.

Bruges may be navigated easily and with great popularity by bicycle. It is effective, economical, cost-effective, fun, and advantageous to your health. On two wheels, visitors may discover the various attractions of the city, take in the beautiful scenery, and discover the special character of Bruges.

## Driving

Lovely Bruges, Belgium, has a fascinating history, lovely buildings, and a quaint medieval vibe. Driving around

Bruges might be a great method to discover this city as it is a well-liked tourist attraction. The benefits and drawbacks of driving in Bruges will be covered in this essay, along with some advice on navigating the city's roadways.

## Benefits of driving in Bruges include:

Convenience: If you are visiting with a family or group of friends, driving around Bruges is incredibly convenient. You are free to pause whenever and wherever you like, and you can effortlessly transport your belongings.

Driving can help you save time because you can travel farther in less time. You can travel to more locations, particularly those that are difficult to reach by public transit.

Comfortable: If you're traveling with young children or the elderly, driving may be a more comfortable option. You don't have to worry about waiting in line or using public transportation, and you can regulate the temperature and music in the car.

Freedom to explore Bruges at your own speed is made possible by driving. You can pick your own path and stop at locations that most interest you. You can also take side trips and tour the city's environs.

## Driving in Bruges has disadvantages

**Parking:** Finding a place to park in Bruges can be difficult, especially in the city center. The majority of the streets are small, and parking is scarce. Finding a good parking location can be challenging, and parking can be pricey.

Bruges can have heavy traffic, particularly during the busiest travel seasons. You can suffer delays as a result of the excessive traffic on the roadways.

**Navigating:** If you are unfamiliar with the city's roadways, navigating Bruges can be difficult. Because some of the streets are curvy and narrow, getting lost can be simple.

# Driving advice for Bruges

**B**efore you start your drive through Bruges, plan your route. To assist you navigate the city's roadways, use a GPS or a map. To prevent the trouble of trying to obtain a parking spot, do some prior research on parking possibilities. In Bruges, there are numerous public parking lots and garages, however they might be pricey.

**Be patient:** During the busiest travel times, be patient and be ready to meet severe traffic. If you can, try to avoid rush hour and allow extra time to get where you're going.

Driving in Bruges requires drivers to pay attention to both cyclists and pedestrians. Be careful not to drive in the city's central streets, which are frequently designated as pedestrian-only zones.

As a result, while driving in Bruges might be a practical and comfortable way to see the city, it also has drawbacks. Your driving experience in Bruges can be improved by preparing your route in advance, looking into parking possibilities, exercising patience, and paying attention to pedestrians and bicycles.

# CHAPTER 3

## Top Bruges Attractions

Bruges, a lovely and endearing city located in the center of Belgium, gives tourists a view of the country's fascinating past, stunning architecture, and mouthwatering cuisine. Bruges, commonly referred to as the Venice of the North, is a well-liked tourist destination because of its abundance of historical and cultural treasures.

Bruges is a treasure trove of attractions that will leave you in amazement, from the renowned belfry tower to the serene canals that weave their way through the city. The major attractions that make Bruges a must-visit location for everyone wishing to experience the finest that Belgium has to offer will be covered in this essay.

## Marketplace Square

In many cities and towns around the world, the Market Square, often referred to as the Town Square, serves as the center of trade and culture.

This dynamic and busy neighborhood is frequently crowded with street performers amusing onlookers, vendors selling regional goods, and people from all walks of life taking in the colorful environment. A trip to the Market Square is a fantastic way for visitors to explore local culture and gain a sense of the distinctive character of the city.

The architecture of the nearby buildings is one of the Market Square's most recognizable aspects. The gorgeous façade and elaborate embellishments on many of these structures, many of them are historical sites and display the city's rich history. Some locations may even have centuries-old structures that offer a look into the past and a sense of the city's history.

A fantastic area to buy gifts and regional goods is the Market Square. The streets are lined with vendors and shops selling anything from fresh meats and veggies to handmade jewelry and crafts.

Visitors can peruse the booths and taste regional treats including cheese, bread, and pastries. In the Market Square of many cities, farmers' markets are also held on a weekly or monthly basis where customers can buy fresh produce, other goods, and other items directly from the growers.

Along with being a place to buy, the Market Square frequently acts as a center for cultural activity. The region is filled with street entertainers and musicians who amuse both locals and visitors. In some cities, the Market Square itself hosts festivals and other events that highlight the local traditions and customs.

These occasions offer a wonderful chance to fully experience the local culture and might range from parades and concerts to wine tastings and cuisine festivals.

The Market Square can also offer a wealth of knowledge about the city's past for those who are interested in it. Many cities provide visitors with in-depth looks at the structures, monuments, and landmarks that have been important to the city's growth through guided tours of the neighborhood.

In some situations, visitors could also be able to go to historical buildings or museums that are situated in or close to Market Square, giving them a fuller insight of the history and culture of the city.

Without eating some of the regional fare, of course, no trip to the Market Square would be complete. The Market Square is certain to offer something to suit your tastes, whether you're searching for a quick snack or a substantial supper.

The Market Square offers a wide range of dining alternatives, from expensive restaurants serving gourmet meals to street sellers selling hot dogs and pretzels. Additionally, visitors can sample regional specialties like cheeses, meats, and wines, which are frequently offered by local vendors.

For those who want to learn about the local way of life and experience the distinctive character of the city, the Markct Square is a must-visit location. The Market Square offers visitors of all ages and interests a memorable experience with its historic architecture, lively ambiance, and broad selection of dining and retail opportunities. As a result, if you're making travel plans to a new city or town, be sure to prioritize visiting the Market Square.

## The Bruges Belfry

One of Belgium's most famous and recognized attractions is the Belfry of Bruges, which is situated in the midst of the old city. This 13th-century medieval tower is more than 80 meters tall and offers breathtaking views of the surroundings. A visit to the Belfry is a must for visitors to Bruges as it provides a fascinating look into the city's rich history and culture.

The ascent to the tower's summit is one of the Belfry's principal draws. The 366-step narrow stairway can be climbed by those who want to see the spectacular panoramic views of the city below. Tourists may view the surrounding countryside as well as Bruges' ancient structures and canals from the top of the tower. On a clear day, it's even possible to view the English Channel's coast.

Visitors can ogle the spectacular bell collection kept in the tower as they ascend the Belfry's stairs. These bells have been booming out over the city for generations, signaling the hour and key events like weddings and funerals. The Belfry houses 47 bells, including a giant 10,000-pound bell known as the "Great Bell."

Visitors can visit the historical rooms and exhibits housed inside the Belfry in addition to ascending the tower. A modest museum on the bells' and tower's history is housed in the tower. The original mechanism that runs the clock face on the tower's exterior is also visible to visitors. One of the oldest operating clock mechanisms in the world, the clock dates to the 17th century and is still in service today.

The annual carillon performances held at the Belfry are a further well-liked feature. A series of bells known as a carillon is played manually by a carillonneur, who manages the bells with a keyboard and pedals. These performances offer a one-of-a-kind chance to hear the Belfry bells in operation and take in Bruges' rich musical legacy.

The Belfry is situated right in the middle of the UNESCO World Heritage Site that encompasses the ancient city core of Bruges. Visitors can stroll through the city's charming streets, visit its art galleries and museums, and savor its world-famous chocolate and beer. Its well-preserved medieval architecture may be seen in structures like the Church of Our Lady and the Groeningemuseum. Bruges is well-known for this.

For visitors to the city, seeing the Belfry of Bruges is a must-do activity. The historical rooms and exhibits within offer a fascinating insight at the tower's fascinating history, and the journey to the top of the tower affords breathtaking views of the surrounding area. The city's well-preserved medieval architecture and the carillon concerts make

Bruges a popular vacation spot for both history and culture lovers. The Belfry of Bruges is a must-see site that shouldn't be missed, regardless of your interest in music, history, or architecture.

## The Our Lady's Church

The Church of Our Lady is one of the most significant and magnificent religious structures in the city of Bruges, Belgium. The church, which honors the Virgin Mary, draws visitors from all over the world with its exquisite architecture and artwork. The Church of Our Lady is a must-see sight for visitors to Bruges and provides a window into the city's rich religious and cultural legacy.

A Gothic-style church built in the 13th century, the Church of Our Lady. The last extensions were added in the 16th century after several centuries of work were completed. With a height of more than 120 meters, the church is renowned for its impressive height. Only the Ulm Minster in Germany is taller than the church's spire, which is the second-tallest brick tower in the world.

The Church of Our Lady is well known for its art collection, which includes numerous significant pieces by well-known Flemish painters. The marble sculpture of Madonna and Child by Michelangelo is the most well-known of these. The sculpture, which was purchased by a wealthy inhabitant of Bruges in the 16th century, is one of only a handful of Michelangelo creations to have left Italy during the artist's lifetime. It now ranks among the most prized pieces of art in the city and attracts tourists from all over the world.

The Church of Our Lady houses several significant sculptures by other Flemish masters in addition to Michelangelo's. These include works by Gerard David, Hans Memling, and Jan van Eyck. A number of magnificent monuments and tributes to famous individuals from Bruges' history, including wealthy businessmen and aristocracy, can also be seen by visitors to the church.

The Church of Our Lady is well known for its magnificent organ. The organ was built in the eighteenth century and has elaborate carvings and ornamental decorations. The organ is still in use today, and it is frequently used for concerts and church services.

Finally, the medieval city center of Bruges, a UNESCO World Heritage Site, is home to the Church of Our Lady. Visitors can stroll through the city's charming streets, visit its art galleries and museums, and savor its world-famous chocolate and beer. Buildings like the Groeningemuseum and the Belfry are examples of Bruges' well-preserved medieval architecture.

Tourists visiting the city should be sure to stop by the Church of Our Lady in Bruges. The church is one of the most significant religious structures in the city and is a top destination for history and culture lovers thanks to its stunning architecture and extensive art collection. It is also situated in the ancient city center. The Church of Our Lady is a must-see destination that shouldn't be missed whether you have an interest in art, history, or religion.

# The Groeninge museum

One of Belgium's most fascinating art museums, the Groeninge Museum is situated in the ancient city of Bruges. All art enthusiasts and travelers curious in the rich cultural heritage of the area must visit this museum. The Groeninge Museum provides a special look into the development of Flemish art over time with its wide collection of works from the 14th century to the present.

The museum is set in a stunning structure that was first used as a monastery and then as a medieval hospital. Early Flemish Primitives through modernist items of art can be found in the museum's collection. Rene Magritte, Hans Memling, Pieter Bruegel the Elder, and other well-known Flemish artists will also have pieces on display, to name a few.

"The Madonna with Canon van der Paele," a painting by Jan van Eyck from 1436, is among the most important pieces in the museum's collection. This picture is a masterpiece of the Northern Renaissance and is regarded as one of the most significant pieces of Flemish art. The elaborate craftsmanship and lifelike representation of the Virgin Mary, who appears to be seated in a church next to a canon, will wow visitors.

Gerard David's "The Judgment of Cambyses" is another masterwork on show. This picture tells the tale of a Persian monarch who murdered his judge after wrongly accusing him. The painting serves as a visual depiction of the moral principle that justice must be administered impartially and honestly. The beautiful painting's rich hues and finely detailed composition can be appreciated by viewers.

A wide range of modern and contemporary works, including creations by Belgian surrealist artist Rene Magritte, are also included in the museum's collection. The museum features "The Empire of Light," one of his most well-known works of art. With its dream-like visuals and provocative subject matter, this work is a great illustration of Magritte's style.

The collection in the Groeninge Museum is not just restricted to paintings. The museum's collection of tapestries, furniture, and sculptures is also open to visitors. The "Six Acts of Mercy," a tapestry from the 16th century, is one of the highlights of the museum's tapestry collection. This tapestry shows six biblical examples of kindness, such as feeding the hungry and covering the naked. Visitors may see the gorgeous piece's meticulous weaving and delicate workmanship.

The Groeninge Museum not only has an outstanding collection, but it also regularly presents temporary exhibitions. Visitors to these shows have the chance to learn more about various artistic movements and styles because they contain works by both national and international artists.

Additionally, the museum offers guided tours that give visitors a more in-depth look at its history and collection. The museum is a great place for students interested in art and history because it also provides educational activities for school groups.

For those who want to learn more about the rich cultural heritage of Bruges and the Flemish region, the Groeninge Museum is a must-see. The museum provides visitors with a distinctive look into the development of Flemish art with its wide collection of paintings from many eras and genres. The Groeninge Museum is a great place to visit and is guaranteed to make an impression, whether you're an art fan or just searching for a diverse cultural experience.

## The Memling Gallery

In the center of Bruges, Belgium—a city renowned for its rich history and gorgeous surroundings—is a hidden jewel called The Memling Museum. The paintings of famed Flemish painter Hans Memling, who is regarded as one of the most important figures of the Northern Renaissance, are the focus of this museum.

The museum is a must-visit location for art and history lovers equally due to its enormous collection of Memling's paintings and other artwork.

The museum may be found inside the venerable Sint-Jan Hospital, which dates back to the 13th century and was a hospital for almost 700 years. The hospital was established by Margareta of Constantinople, Countess of Flanders, and was first devoted to Saint John the Baptist.

During the Middle Ages and the Renaissance, it was one of the most significant hospitals in Europe, and its chapel was renowned for its impressive art collection, which included a number of Memling pieces.

The Memling Museum was founded in the 19th century and is located in a beautifully renovated old hospital ward that has been customized to display Memling's artwork. Some of Memling's most well-known works, including his portraits of Saint Ursula and Saint John the Baptist, as well as a number of religious triptychs and other paintings, are housed in the museum's collection.

The Moreel family triptych, which is regarded as one of Memling's finest, is one of the museum's centerpieces. The triptych features images from Saint Benedict's and Saint

Catherine's lives on the left panel and a wealthy Bruges businessman named Willem Moreel and his family on the center panel. The artwork has great precision and details, and despite being more than 500 years old, the colors are still vivid.

The triptych of the Adoration of the Magi, which was ordered by Florentine banker Tommaso Portinari, is another significant piece in the museum. The painting is renowned for its fine features and vibrant use of color and is regarded as one of the most significant works of art in Bruges. The artwork is evidence of Memling's talent as a painter and his capacity to produce works that are both lovely and significant.

The Memling Museum also houses a collection of sculptures, tapestries, and other ornamental arts from the hospital chapel in addition to the paintings. Visitors can get a glimpse of hospital life through these artworks, as well as learn about the significance of art in the lives of the patients and employees.

Through a number of interactive exhibits and multimedia presentations, the museum also provides visitors with the opportunity to learn more about Memling and the history of the hospital.

With regard to the history of the hospital and the city of Bruges, as well as the life and work of one of the most significant Northern Renaissance artists, these exhibits offer a fascinating look into those periods.

Anyone interested in art, history, or culture must visit the Memling Museum. The paintings and other artworks in the museum's collection by Memling are among the best examples of Northern Renaissance art, and the structure of the museum itself has been wonderfully restored to provide visitors a fascinating look into the past.

The Memling Museum is guaranteed to leave a lasting impact on you, whether you are an experienced art connoisseur or just a casual traveler.

# The Beguinage

The Beguinage, often spelled "béguinage" or "begijnhof," is a special kind of dwelling complex that is mostly found in Belgium and the Netherlands. These complexes, which were initially constructed in the Middle Ages as places for women to live and work together in a religious community, today act as serene getaways for tourists hoping to take in a bit of history.

The first Beguinage was established in the Flemish city of Liège in the 12th century, and during the following several centuries, comparable settlements appeared all across the area. These were frequently started by wealthy patrons who wanted to offer a secure location for women who wished to devote their lives to God without becoming nuns.

The Beguinages were often constructed with separate, modest dwellings, or "béguinages," lining the perimeter of a central courtyard. Each woman had her own room in these modest but cozy dwellings, which also featured a small vegetable garden or plot of ground for gardening.

Despite having a religious focus, beguinages were not as rigidly organized as convents. Although formal religious vows were not required of the women who resided in the Beguinage, they were expected to lead chaste and pious lives. They were required to work as well, either by taking up manual labor like sewing or other types of labor or by providing philanthropic services to the larger community.

The ladies who resided in the Beguinage were subject to a stringent set of rules and regulations notwithstanding their relative freedom and autonomy. They had to adhere to a rigid regimen of work and prayer, as well as daily Mass and other religious services. They also couldn't leave the Beguinage without authorization, and when they did, they had to do it while sporting a recognizable uniform.

The Beguinages developed over time to become hubs of learning and culture. Many of the Beguinage's residents were highly educated women who frequently oversaw educational institutions or worked with young girls from the neighborhood. Many renowned poets, painters, and writers came from the Beguinages, which also served as hubs of artistic and literary creation.

The Beguinages are now used by tourists desiring to immerse themselves in history as serene, secluded getaways. Many of the complexes are in good condition and give visitors a glimpse of life in these settlements hundreds of years ago.

The Begijnhof in Bruges, Belgium, is one of the most well-known Beguinages. This complex, which was built in the thirteenth century, is tucked away in the center of the city and is enclosed by a wall that gives it a sense of isolation and privacy. Visitors to the Begijnhof can stroll around the complex's winding lanes and walkways and take in the béguinages' basic yet magnificent architecture and the serene gardens that surround it.

The Amsterdam Beguinage, which was established in the 14th century, is another noteworthy institution. This

Beguinage is situated in the center of the city and contains a tiny chapel as well as other old structures. The complex is open for visitors to meander through and enjoy while viewing the traditional Dutch architecture and the well-kept gardens.

The Beguinages are an amazing historical site that provide tourists a fascinating look into the life of women who lived hundreds of years ago. In the midst of busy cities, these serene getaways offer a sense of peace and quiet and an opportunity to consider the history and culture of Belgium and the Netherlands. A visit to one of these Beguinages is a must-see whether you are interested in history or are just searching for a quiet getaway.

## The Lake Minne water

In Belgium's ancient city of Bruges, there lies a gorgeous and tranquil lake called the Minne water Lake. It is a well-liked vacation spot renowned for its stunning beauty and serene ambiance. The lake is the ideal location for a tranquil afternoon of reading, a romantic stroll, or a soothing picnic because it is surrounded by thick vegetation.

On the outskirts of the city, the Minne water Lake is conveniently reachable on foot or by bicycle. It is claimed to have been called after a love story involving a knight and a woman who met at the lake. The Dutch term "minne," which means "love," is used as its name. This narrative gives the already lovely surroundings a romantic touch.

There are plenty of opportunities for visitors to soak in the landscape because the lake is encircled by walking pathways and benches. The surrounding trees and foliage make for a lovely backdrop, especially in the fall when the leaves change hues. Additionally, guests can rent a boat and paddle leisurely around the lake while admiring the scenery.

The stunning Gothic-style bridge that crosses the Minne water Lake from the 19th century is one of its features. The bridge, often referred to as the Lovers' Bridge, gives the lake a romantic feel and is a well-liked location for pictures. As a sign of their devotion, visitors can even buy locks to affix to the bridge.

The Poortersloge, a former customs house that now functions as a cultural center, is one of many historic structures that can be found near the Minne water Lake. The structure, which was constructed in the fifteenth century, is a magnificent illustration of Flemish Gothic design. The Kruispoort, one of the original gates of the city of Bruges, is another sight open to visitors. The gate, which was built in the fourteenth century, serves as a reminder of the city's lengthy past.

A number of eateries and cafes can be found all around the lake, giving guests the chance to eat or drink while admiring the lovely surroundings. These restaurants serve a variety of food, including both traditional Belgian meals and other cuisines.

The Minne water Lake is a well-liked location for festivals and activities. The annual Minnewater Festival, a festival of music and dance, is held at the lake every July. All throughout the year, local musicians and artists perform for visitors.

The Minne water Lake is a stunning and tranquil location that tourists to Bruges shouldn't skip. It's the ideal place for a peaceful afternoon or a romantic stroll because to its beautiful surroundings and serene ambience. The lake has something to offer everyone with its historical structures, lovely bridge, and cultural events. A trip to the Minne water Lake is a must-do while in Bruges, whether you're interested in history or just want to unwind.

# CHAPTER 4

## Bruges's Cuisine and Drinks

A center for culture, art, and history is the Flemish section of Belgium's medieval city of Bruges. Visitors to this attractive city are drawn here for many reasons than just the architecture and canals. Bruges' culinary offerings, which include a variety of regional and international cuisines to suit every taste, are equally as appealing.

Belgian culture places a strong emphasis on food and drink, and this is also true of Bruges. The city is well known for its beer, waffles, and chocolate, which are all favorites of both inhabitants and visitors. Bruges offers a wide variety of restaurants, from simple eateries to fine dining establishments with Michelin stars.

The food in Bruges is highly inspired by its close neighbors, France, Germany, and the Netherlands, creating a distinctive mix of tastes. Due to the city's proximity to the

North Sea, fresh fish and shellfish are easily accessible, and seafood plays a big part in the local cuisine.

In addition to its cuisine, Bruges is renowned for its beer. There are innumerable taverns and pubs where visitors can sample some of the famed Belgian beers because the city has a long-standing brewing culture. There is a beer to suit every taste, from delicious lambics to monk-brewed Trappist brews.

Overall, with a wide variety of cuisines and a focus on premium ingredients, Bruges is a foodie's delight. In Bruges, there is something to please every visitor, whether they are a chocolate connoisseur, a seafood enthusiast, or a beer connoisseur. So, if you're thinking of visiting this lovely city, make sure to pack some food and water.

## French Cuisine

Belgium is a small nation in Western Europe that is renowned for its delectable gastronomy, gorgeous architecture, and rich cultural heritage. The culinary traditions of France, the Netherlands, and

Germany have been uniquely and creatively merged to create Belgian cuisine, which is rich, diverse, and appealing to all palates.

Fresh seafood, veggies, and meats are just a few of the premium components that are frequently used in Belgian cuisine. Due to the nation's close proximity to the North Sea, mussels, oysters, and prawns are common ingredients in many recipes. Belgian food is known for its substantial stews, roasts, and sausages that are created with regionally grown meats and produce.

Moules-frites, or mussels with fries, is one of the most well-known Belgian delicacies. White wine and herbs are used to boil the mussels in this dish, which is served with a large serving of crispy French fries. Carbonnade flamande, a hearty beef stew prepared with beer, onions, and mustard, is another well-liked recipe.

Some of the top chocolatiers in the world are from Belgium, which is also well-known for its chocolate. Belgian chocolate is renowned for its smooth, rich texture as well as its wide variety of tastes and fillings. A delicacy of Belgium, pralines are chocolate truffles stuffed with a variety of flavored creams and ganaches. They make the ideal present or keepsake.

Belgium is renowned for its waffles, which are eaten as a snack or dessert in addition to its chocolate. Belgian waffles have a crispy outside and a soft center, and they are thick and fluffy. They are frequently served with whipped cream, powdered sugar, and fresh fruit.

The spiced shortbread cookie known as speculoos, which is typically paired with coffee, is another well-liked sweet treat in Belgium. These cookies have a warm, aromatic flavor that comes from the addition of cinnamon, nutmeg, and cloves.

With a long history of making beer, Belgium is also well known for its beverage. The nation produces a wide variety of beers, ranging from crisp, flavorful pilsners to rich, nuanced Trappist brews made by monks. Belgian beer is often served in its own distinctive glass, with various beer kinds matched with various glass forms.

A rich and varied combination of German, Dutch, and French culinary traditions makes up Belgian cuisine. Everyone may find something they like in Belgian cuisine, from robust stews and seafood to beer and chocolate. Anyone who enjoys fine food and drink should visit Belgium, whether they are foodies or just looking to try something new.

## Renowned Belgian brews

Belgium has a long history of producing beers and is well-known throughout the world for its vast selection of premium brews. Every taste can be satisfied by a Belgian beer, which ranges from crisp and flavorful pilsners to rich and complex Trappist ales. We'll look at some of the most well-known Belgian beers in this essay and what makes them special.

Stella Artois is one of the most well-known beers from Belgium. Stella Artois is a crisp, refreshing lager that was first made in the city of Leuven and is now appreciated all over the world. The smooth, malty flavor and light, hoppy finish of the beer set it apart. It is a traditional Belgian pilsner and frequently served in its distinctive chalice glass.

Duvel, a robust, golden ale made with a high alcohol content of 8.5%, is another well-known Belgian beer. Duvel is surprisingly simple to drink despite its intensity, with a dry, hoppy aftertaste that counteracts the sweetness of the malt. Due to its rich, nuanced flavor and dual fermentation, the beer has become a favorite among beer connoisseurs.

Chimay is a rich and complex beer for those who prefer it. This Trappist beer is renowned for its rich, fruity aroma and nuanced flavor. It is manufactured by monks in a monastery in southern Belgium. There are three main variants of Chimay, with the red label being the most widely available. Because the beer is bottle-conditioned, the yeast is still active inside the bottle, giving it a distinctive and complex flavor.

Westvleteren is another well-known Trappist beer that has spread throughout the world. This beer, which is made by the monks of the Saint Sixtus Abbey in Westvleteren, is regarded as one of the rarest and most coveted in the entire world. It's expensive, hard to get, and there's a strict two-case restriction per person. It's exclusively sold at the monastery. The dark brown beer has a high alcohol concentration of 10.2% and is renowned for its rich, complex flavor.

Along with these well-known brews, Belgium is also well-known for its lambic brews, which are produced utilizing an original fermentation method including wild yeasts and bacteria. These brews have a sour, acidic flavor that is frequently compared to vinegar or sourdough bread. Cantillon, which is brewed in Brussels and is renowned for its distinctive and rich flavor, is one of the most well-known lambic beers.

Some of the most well-known and varied beers in the world come from Belgium. There is a Belgian beer to suit every preference, from traditional pilsners like Stella Artois to sophisticated Trappist ales like Chimay and Westvleteren. Anyone who enjoys good beer should visit Belgium, regardless of whether they are a connoisseur or just curious to try something new.

## Sweets and chocolates

Few locations in the world can match the lovely city of Bruges in Belgium when it comes to chocolate and sweets. Bruges, which has a long tradition of confectionery and chocolate production, is a candy lover's dream come true. This essay will examine the history of chocolate production and confectionery in Bruges, as well as some of the renowned chocolatiers and candy stores that draw gourmands from across the world to the city.

The history of Bruges has long included chocolate. During the Middle Ages, the city was a significant hub of trade, and its travelers to the New World brought back cocoa beans. Since 1850, when Joseph Van Belle founded the city's first chocolate store, Bruges has earned a reputation for producing prcmium chocolate and confections.

Dominique Persoone is among the most well-known chocolatiers in Bruges. His chocolate shop, The Chocolate Line, is noted for its avant-garde and adventurous flavors and is situated in the city's center. Persoone's shop is a must-visit for anyone looking for distinctive and fascinating chocolate creations since he has made chocolates that are infused with anything from bacon to wasabi.

Dumon, which has been producing handcrafted chocolates since 1992, is another well-known chocolatier in Bruges. The historic town center's family-run shop is well-known for its premium ingredients and age-old methods of chocolate production. The process of making beautiful and delectable chocolates is visible to visitors as the chocolatiers work.

There are several of options in Bruges for people who want sweets that aren't made of chocolate. The Old Chocolate House, one of the city's most well-known confectioneries, is renowned for its hot chocolate and waffles. Since it opened in 1981, the store has become a popular among both locals and visitors.

Lizzie's Wafels, another well-known candy store in Bruges, offers typical Belgian waffles with a selection of toppings. The store is a nice place to stop for a sweet treat while touring the city and is only a short stroll from the well-known Markt plaza.

For anyone with a sweet craving, Bruges offers a wide variety of other options in addition to these well-known chocolatiers and confectioneries. There are plenty of options in this attractive city, whether you want classic Belgian chocolates or cutting-edge and unusual varieties.

In conclusion, Bruges is a haven for sweets and chocolate lovers. The city is home to some of the top chocolatiers and candy stores in the world and has a long tradition of producing chocolate and confections. If you enjoy chocolate or are simply looking for a sweet treat, a trip to Bruges will surely sate your appetite.

# CHAPTER 5

## Shopping in Bruges

Bruges offers a unique experience when it comes to shopping. This attractive medieval city is well-known for its historic buildings, picturesque canals, and cobbled streets, but it's also a haven for consumers looking for distinctive and high-quality goods. Bruges has a large selection of goods that make excellent gifts or mementos, ranging from delicate lacework to handcrafted chocolates.

The city's historic district is teeming with stores offering everything from fashionable clothing and accessories to classic Belgian chocolates. Visitors can take a leisurely stroll along the winding alleys and peruse the several boutique stores that line the path while taking in the stunning window displays and distinctive things for sale.

Steenstraat, which connects the Markt square to the city's outer ring, is one of Bruges' most well-known shopping avenues. Visitors can shop for apparel, shoes, and accessories at a variety of high-end designer stores as well as smaller independent businesses.

Numerous artisanal stores in Bruges sell handmade items for those looking for something truly one-of-a-kind. De Witte Pelikaan, a lace store that has been in business since 1898, is one of the most well-known. Visitors can peruse the complex lacework for sale, which includes delicate handkerchiefs and magnificent tablecloths, and see the lacemakers at work.

Dille & Kamille is another well-known artisanal store in Bruges that offers a variety of cookware, home décor, and other products manufactured from natural materials. The store is an excellent choice for people looking for environmentally friendly presents because of its reputation for high-quality goods and dedication to sustainability.

Naturally, a trip to one of the many chocolate shops in Bruges is a must for any trip there. There are plenty of options in this city, from conventional Belgian chocolates to cutting-edge and unusual flavors. A variety of premium chocolates from well-known chocolatiers like Dominique Persoone and Dumon make wonderful gifts and keepsakes.

One should not pass up the opportunity to shop in Bruges. This city has something to offer everyone, whether you're seeking for luxury clothing, artisanal lacework, or mouthwatering chocolates. Therefore, the next time you visit Bruges, make sure to set aside some time for shopping and discover the distinctive and exquisite shops that help to define this special city.

## Souvenirs

Millions of tourists visit the picturesque medieval city of Bruges each year. The city is well-known for its charming canals, ancient structures, and cobbled alleys, but it's also a terrific spot to find distinctive and premium mementos to bring home. Bruges provides a variety of goods that make wonderful gifts and lasting memories, from delectable chocolates to delicate lacework.

Chocolate is among the most recognizable keepsakes from Bruges. Bruges is no different from the rest of Belgium in being known for its chocolate.

In the city, there are numerous chocolate shops that sell everything from conventional Belgian chocolate to novel and experimental flavors. Dumon and Dominique Persoone, two of the most well-known chocolatiers in Bruges, provide premium chocolates that are ideal as presents or for treating oneself.

Beer is another well-liked memento in Bruges. Bruges is home to several regional breweries and bars. Belgium is well-known for its beer culture. From crisp and light pilsners to dark and nuanced Trappist beers, visitors can enjoy a variety of brews.

De Halve Maan, which makes the well-known Brugse Zot beer, and Bourgogne des Flandres, which specializes in Flemish red-brown ale, are two of the most well-known breweries in Bruges.

Bruges is home to a multitude of artisanal businesses selling handmade goods for people looking for something more distinctive. De Witte Pelikaan, a lace store that has been in business since 1898, is one of the most well-known. Visitors can peruse the complex lacework for sale, which includes delicate handkerchiefs and magnificent tablecloths, and see the lacemakers at work.

Other well-known artisanal stores in Bruges include Atelier Rebul, which specializes in high-quality perfumes and cosmetics, and Dille & Kamille, which offers a selection of natural home furnishings and kitchenware.

The city of Bruges is known for its ceramics, and tourists may find a variety of pottery and porcelain items there. For those seeking handcrafted ceramics, the De Roos pottery factory is a well-known stop, and the Keramiek en Porselein Atelier has a selection of exquisite porcelain goods like teapots, cups, and saucers.

Of course, a trip to Bruges wouldn't be complete without bringing home a memento of the city's distinctive charm.

From postcards and posters to small replicas of the city's well-known monuments, visitors may find a variety of things that honor the city's history and culture. Along with these items, the Bruges Lace Center also sells doilies, handkerchiefs, and bookmarks made of lacework.

Bruges is a fantastic location to find one-of-a-kind, top-notch souvenirs. The city provides a variety of products that make for wonderful gifts and memories, from mouthwatering chocolates and beer to handcrafted lacework and pottery. So when you visit Bruges again, make sure to set aside some time to browse the numerous exquisite shops that contribute to this city's unique charm.

## Boutiques

Even though Bruges is a medieval city, it's a terrific place to buy for clothing and accessories. The city is home to a variety of high-end boutiques, vintage stores, and local designers, providing fashion aficionados with a selection of distinctive and trendy options.

The old city center is one of the best places to go shopping for clothes. Visitors can discover a variety of designer shops and global names, such Ralph Lauren, Dior, and Gucci, here. High-end apparel, shoes, and accessories may be found in abundance in the streets around the Markt plaza, which is a particularly well-liked destination for fashion shoppers.

Bruges is also home to a number of regional designers and independent boutiques for those looking for something more distinctive. La Vie en Rose is one such store that sells a variety of women's apparel and accessories that are all created in Bruges. Juttu is a well-known independent store that carries a number of ethical and sustainable clothing labels, such as Patagonia and Stella McCartney.

Several vintage stores in Bruges provide a variety of clothing and accessories from various eras, making vintage shopping a popular activity there as well. Think Twice is one of the most well-known vintage stores in Bruges and has multiple sites throughout the city. Visitors can get everything they need here, from retro footwear and accessories to vintage gowns and coats.

The textile sector in Bruges is also well-known, and many regional designers focus on handcrafted textiles and fabrics. One such designer is Katrien Van Hecke, who uses conventional textile techniques to produce distinctive apparel and accessories. Her creations are sold in the Katrien Van Hecke store in Bruges.

In addition to selling clothing and accessories, Bruges is a fantastic place to buy jewelry. Numerous jewelry designers and stores with a variety of distinctive and fashionable pieces can be found in the city. Ann Demeulemeester is one such designer, and she makes sleek, contemporary jewelry that draws inspiration from her clothing collections. Juwelen Henri Dom is a well-known jewelry store in Bruges that specialized in antique and vintage jewelry.

Last but not least, a trip to Bruges for fashion and accessory shopping would be incomplete without stopping by one of the city's renowned lace stores. Visitors can discover a variety of lace goods, including shawls, scarves, and blouses, at the Bruges Lace Center and various lace stores across the city. Bruges is recognized for its elaborate and delicate lacework.

Even though Bruges is a historic city, it's a terrific place to buy for clothing and accessories. In Bruges, there is something for every type and taste, including high-end brand boutiques, independent local designers, vintage stores, and traditional lace shops. So, if you're a fan of fashion, make sure to put Bruges on your travel itinerary and peruse the city's many exquisite and distinctive clothing boutiques.

## Regional goods

Shopping in Bruges is about more than simply fashion and trinkets. The region is renowned for its locally produced goods, which are crafted using premium ingredients and time-honored methods. Visitors can find a variety of regional goods to bring home as a delectable and distinctive memento of their journey to

Bruges, from cheese and beer to chocolate and beer to cheese and handcrafted soap.

Chocolate is among the most well-known regional goods in Bruges. Bruges is home to a number of chocolate stores and chocolatiers that offer a variety of delectable and attractive chocolates. Belgium is famed for its high-quality chocolate.

The Chocolate Line, one of the most well-known chocolate stores in Bruges, sells a variety of inventive and artistic chocolates with flavors like wasabi, bacon, and curry. Dumon Chocolatier, which has been producing handmade chocolates since 1992 using only the best ingredients, is another well-known chocolate shop in Bruges.

Bruges is well-known not only for its chocolate but also for its beer. De Halve Maan and Bourgogne des Flandres are two of the many regional breweries that call Bruges home. Belgium has a long and proud history of brewing. In Bruges, a variety of regional beers are available, including robust and dark Trappist ales and sweet lambics. Beer enthusiasts can also go to the Bruges Beer Museum to learn about Belgian beer's history and enjoy a variety of regional beers.

Another regional good available to tourists in Bruges is cheese. Belgium still makes some wonderful and distinctive sorts of cheese, even though it may not be as well known for it as France or the Netherlands are. Brugge Kaas, a semi-hard cheese with a creamy and slightly sweet flavor, is one of the most well-known Belgian cheeses. The Cheese Board and Kaasmarkt are only two of the city's many cheese stores where tourists may purchase Brugge Kaas and other regional cheeses.

Another regional good that may be purchased by tourists in Bruges is handmade soap. There are various soap stores in the city that sell a variety of bath goods and handcrafted soaps. The Soap Story, one of the most well-known soap businesses in Bruges, offers a variety of vibrant and fragrant soaps that are crafted utilizing conventional techniques and natural materials.

L'Occitane en Provence, which offers a variety of opulent and fragrant bath and body products inspired by the south of France, is another well-known soap shop in Bruges.

Last but not least, Bruges is renowned for its delicate lacework, which is created using age-old methods. In Bruges, a variety of lace goods, such as doilies, tablecloths, and shawls, are available for purchase. The Bruges Lace Center is one of the best sites in Bruges to buy lace. Here, customers may buy handcrafted lace items and observe lace craftsmen at work.

In Bruges, buying regional goods is a wonderful opportunity to experience the city's renowned and excellent craftsmanship. Visitors can purchase a variety of distinctive and delectable goods to take home as a memento of their stay to Bruges, including cheese, beer, chocolate, and lace. So make sure to browse the city's numerous independent stores and boutiques to find the delicious and exquisite goods that Bruges has to offer.

# CHAPTER 6

## Accommodation in Bruges

Bruges, a well-liked tourist destination, provides guests with a selection of lodging choices, from opulent hotels to inviting bed & breakfasts. Bruges is the perfect destination for a romantic weekend or a family holiday because of its charming cobblestone streets, historical structures, and picturesque canals.

The medieval hotel is one of the most popular types of lodging in Bruges. Many of the city's historic structures have been transformed into opulent hotels, giving guests the opportunity to experience the city's rich history while taking advantage of contemporary amenities.

The Hotel Heritage, which is built in a 19th-century palace and offers exquisite accommodations, a Michelin-starred restaurant, and a spa, is one of the most well-known historic hotels in Bruges. The Grand Hotel Casselbergh, the

Hotel de Tuilerieen, and the Hotel Jan Brito are more Bruges ancient inns.

## Hotels

Bruges, a well-known tourist attraction, provides a selection of hotels to meet the requirements of every guest. For visitors wishing to experience the lovely city of Bruges, there is no shortage of lodging choices, from opulent five-star hotels to affordable alternatives.

The Hotel Heritage is among the most renowned and opulent hotels in Bruges. This hotel, housed in a magnificently restored 19th-century estate, offers superb rooms and suites embellished with priceless antiques. The hotel's Michelin-starred restaurant, inviting bar, and tranquil spa, which offers a sauna, steam room, and massage treatments, are all available to guests.

The Grand Hotel Casselbergh is another renowned luxury hotel in Bruges. The spacious rooms and suites of this historic hotel, which is centrally positioned, offer stunning views of the city's historic district. The hotel's spa facility, which includes a sauna, Turkish bath, and workout room, as well as the little bar and restaurant, are available to guests.

There are also some mid-range and low-cost hotels in Bruges for visitors seeking a more affordable lodging alternative. The NH Brugge is a well-liked option since it provides cozy accommodations and a great position just a short stroll from the city center. Another mid-range choice is the Hotel Aragon, which has comfortable accommodations and a tranquil garden terrace.

Bruges also has a variety of boutique hotels for visitors who desire a more distinctive and exclusive experience. A stunning structure from the 15th century that has been converted into a posh boutique hotel is called the Hotel De Orangerie. The hotel offers classy guestrooms and suites with lovely canal views, as well as a delightful garden terrace and a welcoming bar.

In addition to conventional hotels, Bruges also provides a number of unique lodging options. The Boat Hotel De Barge is an opulent barge that is moored in the city's canals. It offers comfortable cabins and suites with stunning river views. Another interesting choice is the Martin's Relais Hotel, which is built in a heritage structure and features opulent rooms with antique decor and a lovely courtyard garden.

In conclusion, Bruges provides a variety of lodging options to meet the requirements of every visitor. Bruges features lodging options for every price range, whether you're seeking for a five-star resort or a modest lodging alternative.

Bruges is the ideal location for a romantic trip, a family holiday, or a single adventure because of its lovely old buildings, gorgeous canals, and fantastic food and shopping opportunities. In order to discover the ideal lodging for your vacation to Bruges, be sure to look through the city's numerous hotels.

# Overnight accommodations

Bed and breakfasts (B&Bs) are a popular option for tourists seeking a more personal and distinctive experience in Bruges. These lodging options provide a personalized touch and the opportunity to stay in old homes with a cozy atmosphere.

There are a variety of B&Bs in Bruges, from charming and comfortable to opulent and fashionable. Many of these B&Bs are housed in old structures that have charming elements like stained-glass windows, beamed ceilings, and exposed brick walls.

The Bonifacius Guesthouse is among the top B&Bs in Bruges. This opulent B&B is based in a revered 16th-century structure that is situated in the center of the city. Six magnificent rooms and suites are available at the inn, each of which is furnished with a different antique and work of art. A complementary breakfast is available to guests in the inviting dining room or on the terrace garden that looks out into the canal.

The Canal Deluxe Bed & Breakfast, housed in a stunning 17th-century structure with views of Bruges' gorgeous canals, is another well-known B&B. The B&B offers four beautiful, roomy accommodations, each with a private bathroom and contemporary conveniences.

A delectable breakfast is served in the dining room or on the garden patio, and guests are welcome to utilize the hotel's complimentary bicycles to explore the city.

Budget-conscious tourists can also find a number of comfortable and reasonably priced B&B options in Bruges. Just a short stroll from the city center, the Huyze Weyne Bed & Breakfast is a charming inn housed in a typical 19th-century structure.

The inn has four inviting rooms, each with a distinctive design and modern conveniences like free Wi-Fi and a flat-screen TV. A continental breakfast is available to guests in the inviting dining room or on the garden patio.

The Guesthouse De Roode, housed in a historic structure and approximately ten minutes' walk from the city center, is another budget-friendly choice. Four comfortable, colorful rooms with contemporary facilities are available at this B&B, together with a shared parlor and kitchenette. A delectable breakfast is offered to guests in the dining room or on the garden terrace.

In addition to these well-liked B&Bs, Bruges provides a variety of other quaint and distinctive lodging options. There is a B&B in Bruges that will meet your demands, whether you're seeking for an opulent and fashionable stay or a comfortable and economical choice.

Travelers seeking to discover the city of Bruges can have a special and exclusive experience at a bed and breakfast. B&Bs provide a cozy atmosphere that is unmatched by typical hotels because to their lovely historical structures, unique embellishments, and delectable breakfasts. Search through the many bed and breakfast establishments in Bruges to find the ideal place to stay for your visit to this stunning city.

# Vacation rentals and apartments

Apartments and holiday rentals are excellent choices for visitors seeking more room and independence while visiting Bruges. These lodgings provide the chance to experience local life while discovering the city's lovely streets, canals, and architecture.

From tiny studios to roomy family flats, Bruges has a range of apartments and holiday rentals to suit all types of guests. Many of these lodgings are housed in old structures with distinctive characteristics like exposed brick walls, beamed ceilings, and elaborate facades.

The Holiday Suites company, one of the most well-known vacation rental firms in Bruges, provides a variety of contemporary and cozy apartments in ideal locations all throughout the city. These residences have modern furnishings, a full kitchen, and separate bathrooms. For a small cost, visitors can use the hotel's services, including the fitness center, sauna, and daily breakfast buffet.

Airbnb is a well-liked alternative that provides a variety of flats and holiday rentals in Bruges. Travelers can choose from a wide range of distinctive and appealing lodgings to meet their needs, from tiny studios to roomy lofts. These accommodations give guests the chance to stay in nearby communities with hosts who can provide advice on how to explore the city.

In Bruges, there are also a number of roomy vacation apartments accessible for families or bigger parties. For instance, the City Center flats in Bruges have a variety of flats that may house up to six people. In addition to having a full kitchen, living room, and dining space, these apartments also have contemporary conveniences like free Wi-Fi and a flat-screen TV.

In addition to these well-liked choices, Bruges also has a wide selection of distinctive and endearing holiday rentals, including houseboats and old townhouses. For instance, The Houseboat Mermaid is a quaint and eccentric holiday rental situated on a tranquil canal just a short stroll from the city center. This houseboat features a living area, kitchen, and bathroom in addition to a private balcony with canal views.

In general, Bruges' flats and vacation rentals provide visitors who want to explore the city at their own leisure with a distinctive and independent experience. These lodgings provide a home away from home in one of Europe's most attractive and picturesque cities thanks to their unique touches and cozy conveniences. So, be sure to look through all of Bruges' available apartments and vacation rentals to find the ideal place to stay during your visit to this stunning city.

# CHAPTER 7

## Bruges day trips

B ruges is a lovely and gorgeous city, but there are also a lot of places to visit close by. There are numerous day trips you can take from Bruges to neighboring cities, villages, and attractions, depending on your interests—whether they are in history, the outdoors, or just a change of pace.

Visitors to Bruges have access to a wide range of fun and interesting day trip choices. There is something nearby this quaint city for everyone, whether you're looking for history, culture, nature, or just a change of pace.

## Ghent

Just a short train ride from Bruges is the lively and historic city of Ghent. Ghent, known for its spectacular architecture, vibrant cultural scene, and picturesque canals, provides the ideal counterpoint to Bruges' more subdued charm. Consider making a day trip to Ghent from Bruges so that you can experience this vibrant city and all of its sights and activities.

Ghent's magnificent architecture is one of its most noticeable characteristics. The city's historical structures are a monument to its rich history and culture, from the soaring spires of St. Bavo's Cathedral to the Gothic-style Castle of the Counts. Visitors can explore the city's various landmarks and learn about its intriguing history by going on a walking tour.

The thriving cultural scene of Ghent is another reason to visit. The city is home to numerous galleries, museums, and cultural organizations, such as the Ghent City Museum, the Design Museum, and the Museum of Fine Arts. The city's vibrant music and theater scenes can be explored by visitors in addition to the numerous exhibitions and events that are held throughout the year.

Ghent is renowned for its attractive canals as well, which snake through the city and provide an interesting perspective on its landscape and architectural features. Visitors can experience the city from a fresh perspective and take in the breathtaking surroundings by taking a boat trip of the canals.

Foodies will also adore Ghent because of the city's reputation for superb cuisine. Every palate can find something to enjoy in Ghent, from modern restaurants and cafes to traditional Belgian waffles and chocolate. Visitors can savor some of the regional fare, unwind at one of the city's many breweries, or simply sample some of the local cuisine.

In general, anyone traveling to the area must take a day trip from Bruges to Ghent. Ghent is a city that is guaranteed to win the hearts of everyone who visit with its magnificent architecture, lively culture, attractive canals, and delectable cuisine.

The capital of Belgium, Brussels, is among the most well-known and cosmopolitan cities in all of Europe. The best way to experience Brussels' history, culture, and culinary delights is on a day trip from Bruges.

The Atomium, a mammoth edifice created for the 1958 World Expo, is one of Brussels' most well-known landmarks. The Atomium is open for tours, and from its observation deck, guests may take in sweeping panoramas of the city. The Manneken Pis, a diminutive statue of a kid peeing that has come to represent the city, is another well-known sight.

The Royal Museums of Fine Arts of Belgium, the Magritte Museum, and the Museum of the City of Brussels are just a few of the museums and galleries that can be found in Brussels. Visitors can explore the numerous exhibitions and activities that are held all year long and discover the city's rich history and culture.

Brussels is renowned for its delectable gastronomy and renowned culinary offerings, and foodies will adore it. Visitors can experience these regional delicacies in a number of eateries, cafes, and shops because the city is known for its chocolate, beer, and waffles. Additionally, there are many Michelin-starred restaurants in Brussels where tourists can sample some of the best food on earth.

Shopping lovers will also adore Brussels, which has several different shopping areas and markets. While the Sablon neighborhood is well-known for its antique stores and art galleries, the Avenue Louise is known for its upscale clothing boutiques and luxury stores. The Marolles Flea Market is a well-liked stop for tourists looking for uncommon trinkets and antiques.

Overall, anyone traveling to the area must take a day trip from Bruges to Brussels. Brussels is a city that is likely to enthrall tourists of all interests and backgrounds with its renowned landmarks, vibrant culture, delectable cuisine, and fantastic shopping choices.

# Antwerp

Just one hour from Bruges, the vibrant and historic city of Antwerp makes for a great day trip. Antwerp is a city that has plenty to offer for everyone with its fascinating history, beautiful architecture, and fantastic shopping and culinary opportunities.

The Cathedral of Our Lady, a magnificent Gothic church from the 14th century, is one of Antwerp's top attractions. The spectacular interior of the cathedral can be explored by guests, and it is decorated with artwork by well-known artists like Rubens and Van Dyck. The Antwerp Central Station, which is regarded as one of the most magnificent train stations in the world, is another must-see destination.

Because Antwerp is a center for the diamond industry, the city is renowned for its fantastic shopping opportunities as well. Visitors who want to buy diamonds or just enjoy the exquisite jewelry on exhibit frequently go to the Diamond District. Along with a bustling market where tourists can buy local goods and souvenirs, the city is also home to a number of hip boutiques and designer stores.

Antwerp, which is renowned for its delectable gastronomy and culinary traditions, will also appeal to foodies. The Flemish stew, a substantial meat dish cooked in beer and eaten with bread and mustard, is the city's claim to fame. At a variety of eateries and cafes, visitors can also sample regional specialties like waffles, chocolates, and Belgian beer.

The Rubens House, a museum devoted to the life and works of the well-known Flemish artist Peter Paul Rubens, is another well-liked site in Antwerp. A substantial collection of Rubens' paintings, as well as his personal effects and works by his contemporaries, are on display in the museum.

Overall, visiting Antwerp for the day from Bruges is a wonderful way to learn about the distinctive culture and history of this stunning city. Antwerp is a city that should not be missed because of its gorgeous architecture, fantastic dining and shopping opportunities, and rich creative and cultural legacy.

## Belgium's Coast

The Belgian seaside is a fantastic choice for a tranquil day excursion from Bruges. The coast is only a short drive away and is home to several charming seaside towns, stunning beaches, and mouthwatering seafood eateries.

The town of Knokke-Heist, which is renowned for its luxury boutiques, art galleries, and hip cafes, is one of the most visited locations along the Belgian coast. The town's picturesque streets may be explored, the beach promenade can be strolled along, and local specialties like fresh oysters and mussels can be enjoyed.

The town of Ostend, which is renowned for its sandy beaches, vibrant boardwalk, and old buildings, is another must-see location along the coast. Swim in the North Sea, visit the town's art galleries and museums, or just unwind at one of the many coastal cafes.

The town of De Haan is an excellent alternative if you want a more private and serene beach experience. The picturesque dunes, lovely houses, and tranquil ambiance of this little village are well-known. Visitors can stroll around the town's parks and gardens, have a leisurely bike ride down the coast, or just rest on the beach while it's sunny.

Without trying some of the renowned seafood the area is known for, a vacation to the Belgian coast would be incomplete. Numerous top-notch seafood establishments can be found along the coast, where patrons can savor the day's freshest catches of lobster, crab, and shrimp.

An excellent way to get away from the city and enjoy some sun, sand, and sea is to take a day trip from Bruges to the Belgian coast. The coast is a must-visit location because of its attractive seaside villages, stunning beaches, and mouthwatering seafood.

# CHAPTER 8

## Useful Information

In Belgium's Flemish region sits the lovely and ancient city of Bruges. It is a well-liked destination for tourists from all over the world due to its scenic canals, lovely cobblestone alleys, and spectacular architecture.

It is crucial to keep some useful information in mind while making travel plans to Bruges if you want to make the most of your experience. Overall, visitors can fully enjoy everything that Bruges has to offer, from its rich history and culture to its beautiful scenery and mouthwatering cuisine, by keeping a few useful tips in mind.

## Visitor Information Centers

A tourist information office is one of the most valuable resources for visitors to a new city or nation. These businesses offer useful details about events, lodging options, and transportation in the area. There are numerous tourist information centers in Bruges that can assist visitors in making the most of their trip.

The Historium, a well-known museum that provides a multimedia experience about the history of the city, is where the major tourist information center is situated in Bruges.

Every day from 10 am to 5 pm, the office is open and offers a variety of services, including maps and brochures, information on events and attractions, and assistance in making travel and lodging arrangements. Additionally, multilingual staff members who speak English, French, German, Spanish, Italian, and Dutch are on hand to help visitors.

There are numerous other tourist information offices spread out over the city in addition to the main office. One of these is an office at the train station, which is open from Monday through Saturday from 9 a.m. to 6 p.m. and from 9 a.m. to 2 p.m. on Sundays and holidays. At the Belfry, there is a separate office that is open Monday through Friday from 10 am to 5 pm.

The provision of a city card is one distinctive feature of the tourist information centers in Bruges. The Bruges City Card offers discounts on tours, transportation, and dining as well as free admission to several of the city's famous attractions. The card can be purchased at any of the tourist information centers and is offered for several time frames, ranging from 48 to 72 hours.

The Visit Bruges app, which is free to download for iOS and Android smartphones, is another useful tool for tourists. The app offers details about nearby sights to see, activities to attend, and restaurants, in addition to interactive maps and audio tours for self-guided excursions.

In general, visitors to the city can benefit from the services offered by Bruges' tourist information centers. Travelers may be sure they will have all the information they need to make the most of their vacation to this stunning and historic city thanks to the staff's friendliness and expertise, as well as the variety of services on offer.

## Security and Safety

B ruges is a well-known tourist attraction that draws millions of travelers every year from all over the world. Despite the fact that the city is usually thought to be secure, visitors should nonetheless be aware of security and safety threats to ensure a smooth and pleasurable visit. This essay will go over some important security and safety tips for visitors to Bruges.

The most crucial safety advice for visitors to Bruges is to be on the lookout for theft and pickpocketing. This is particularly true in popular tourist locations like the Markt and the Burg, where pickpockets may prey on unwary visitors.

Keep your belongings close to hand at all times, and be aware of your surroundings, to prevent becoming a victim of theft. For instance, never leave your suitcase unsecured in a public location, and be on the lookout for anyone acting strangely or approaching you too closely.

Traffic safety is another issue of worry for tourists in Bruges. Despite the city's tiny size and accessibility by foot or bicycle, visitors should nevertheless use caution when cycling or crossing streets. Use marked pedestrian crossings at all times, and heed traffic signals. The local traffic laws and restrictions should also be understood by visitors who opt to rent bicycles.

Tourists should be mindful of the threat of terrorism throughout Europe, notably in Belgium, in terms of security. Although Bruges is unlikely to experience a terrorist attack, it is still crucial to be cautious and aware of your surroundings. Report anything strange or unusual to the police right away if you notice it.

Additionally, tourists should be aware of the possibility of fraud and scams in Bruges. bogus "official" tour guides and street sellers peddling bogus items are two common tourist traps. It's crucial to conduct thorough research in advance and only work with reliable tour operators and suppliers to prevent being a victim of these frauds. Tourists should also be cautious of anyone who approaches them on the street with an unbelievable offer.

Last but not least, travelers should be mindful of the possibility of natural disasters like flooding. Due to its low elevation, Bruges is susceptible to flooding during downpours or storms. It's crucial to stay up to date on weather forecasts and heed any evacuation orders issued by local authorities if you want to stay safe during a flood.

Visitors should be aware of the different safety and security threats even though Bruges is generally regarded as a safe and secure tourist destination. Tourists may contribute to ensuring a safe and happy visit to this lovely city by taking simple precautions like being aware of your surroundings, keeping your possessions close to you, and utilizing designated pedestrian crossings and traffic signals.

# Money and Tipping

To avoid any confusion or misunderstandings while visiting Bruges, it is crucial to have a basic awareness of the local currency and tipping practices. In this post, we'll go over some important things visitors to Bruges should know about money and tipping.

## Currency:

The Euro is the official currency of Bruges and all of Belgium. It is significant to note that most businesses in Bruges, including restaurants, hotels, and shops, accept credit and debit cards. But it's always a good idea to have some cash on hand for smaller purchases and for locations where cards are not accepted.

When using credit or debit cards outside of the country, it's also crucial to be aware of exchange rates and costs. To prevent any problems with transactions being stopped, it is advised to inform your bank or credit card provider in advance of your vacation intentions.

**Tipping:**

Generally speaking, tipping is not as common or expected in Bruges as it is in other nations, like the US. In restaurants, cafes, and bars, it is still customary to round up the total or leave a modest tip of 10% or less for good service. This is especially true for more premium places where better service is anticipated.

Additionally, it is typical to give small gratuities to hotel staff members like housekeepers and bellhops for their assistance. Depending on the quality of the service, the tip size may change.

It is significant to emphasize that other service providers, such as cab drivers, hairdressers, and spa attendants, do not anticipate tips. However, it is always appreciated to express your gratitude with a small tip if you receive exceptional service or go above and beyond what is expected.

It's critical to remain alert to any potential frauds or unstated charges when it comes to currency exchange. Instead of exchanging money with street vendors or in tourist locations, it is advised to do so at banks or authorized exchange offices.

It's also critical to understand the worth of Belgian coins and currency. Along with 1 and 2 Euro coins and smaller coin denominations, the Euro is available in bills with the following denominations: 5, 10, 20, 50, 100, 200, and 500. Getting acquainted with the currency in advance can help you complete transactions without confusion.

Tourists should take time to research local money and tipping practices before traveling to Bruges. Tourists can assure a pleasant and trouble-free trip while admiring the lovely city of Bruges by understanding the Euro currency and its denominations, using credit and debit cards, tipping appropriately for services, and exchanging money at authorized outlets.

## Culture and Language

With its own distinct language and customs, Bruges is a city rich in culture and history. It is crucial for tourists to comprehend these cultural facets in order to respect and fully appreciate the customs of the host country. This post will go over some important things tourists should know about the language and traditions in Bruges.

## Language:

Belgian has three official languages: Dutch, French, and German, with Dutch being the main tongue in Bruges. However, the majority of establishments, including hotels, restaurants, and shops, as well as tourist hotspots, speak English. As a demonstration of respect for the native tongue, it is advised to learn a few fundamental Dutch expressions like "Dank u wel" (thank you), "Alstublieft" (please), and "Goedemorgen" (good morning).

The use of several languages by Belgians varies depending on the circumstance or the person they are conversing with. For instance, people might speak English in tourist regions to accommodate foreign guests. However, they might favor speaking in Dutch or French in more formal or professional settings.

## Customs:

Many traditions and customs from Belgium's rich history and culture are still followed today. It is crucial for tourists to be aware of and respectful of these traditions. The following are some Bruges traditions:

Belgians cherish being on time and see it as a show of respect. For appointments or meetings, it's critical to be on time.

Dress code: Proper attire is expected in more formal contexts, such as business meetings or fine dining establishments. For both men and women, this can entail donning a suit and tie.

Belgians have particular habits when it comes to dining and take their food seriously. For instance, it is traditional to finish the food on your plate, keep your hands on the table, and place your napkin on your lap during the meal.

Belgians place a high priority on courteous and respectful greetings. Depending on the level of acquaintance, it is usual to greet someone with a handshake or a kiss on either cheek. Using a person's title and last name is advised in more formal contexts, such as business meetings.

festivals: There are numerous national festivals and customs in Belgium, including the well-known Christmas markets in Bruges and the Carnival of Binche. It's crucial to respect the traditions and practices connected to these holidays and to be aware of them.

Travel planning for tourists should include learning the local language and traditions in Bruges. Tourists can demonstrate their admiration for the history and culture of this stunning city by using the native language and customs with respect.

# CONCLUSION

With its gorgeous architecture, extensive history, and distinctive culture, Bruges is a city that enthralls tourists. There are numerous activities to see and do in Bruges, a well-liked tourist attraction, including strolling around the city's narrow streets and canals and visiting museums and art galleries. In this travel guide, we've covered a few important things to think about before visiting Bruges.

When traveling to any destination, safety and security must come first. It's critical to pay attention to your surroundings, take safety measures to secure your possessions, and abide by local laws and ordinances.

Travelers should be aware of the currency exchange rates and costs as well as the norms for tipping at restaurants and hotels when it comes to money and tipping. In order to avoid frauds, it's also crucial to understand the worth of Belgian coins and bills and to only exchange money at places that are authorized to do so.

Traveling to Bruges also requires consideration of the local language and customs. As a demonstration of respect for the native tongue, it is advised to learn some fundamental Dutch words even though English is frequently spoken in tourist regions. Tourists should also be aware of the traditions surrounding greetings, punctuality, clothing code, and eating etiquette.

Last but not least, Bruges is a city rich in history and culture, with many distinctive traditions and customs. Tourists should respect and value these traditions, be aware of regional celebrations and customs, and have a genuine and respectful experience of the city.

Visitors can have a one-of-a-kind and amazing trip in Bruges. By being aware of these important factors, visitors may take advantage of everything the city has to offer while also respecting the traditions and culture of the area. Bruges is a city that will leave a lasting impact on everyone who visits, from the gorgeous architecture to the rich history and distinctive traditions.

T here are a lot of things travelers can do to make their trip to Bruges pleasant and pleasurable. There are a number of extra suggestions that might help travelers get the most out of their time in this lovely city in addition to the factors included in this travel guide.

**Plan ahead:** To ensure that you have enough time to see and do everything you want to, it is crucial to plan your vacation well in advance. This entails making advance reservations for lodging, travel, and events to reduce stress at the last minute.

Bruges is a relatively tiny city, but the meandering streets and alleyways make it simple to get lost. Get a map. You can navigate more effectively and prevent getting lost if you get a map of the city and become familiar with its layout.

**Take a walking tour:** this is the best way to experience Bruges. A local guide can provide you insightful information about the history and culture of the city while pointing out hidden jewels that you might have missed on your own.

**Try the local cuisine:** From beer and moules-frites (mussels and fries) to chocolate and waffles, Belgium is recognized for its delectable gastronomy. Experiencing local cuisine and beverages is essential to understanding Bruges' culture.

**Visit off-the-beaten-path attractions:** Bruges has many lesser-known attractions that are just as fascinating as the city's well-known tourist attractions. For instance, although it is off the usual road, the Beguinage is a serene and attractive convent that is worth a visit.

**Be respectful:** It's crucial to respect the local customs and culture everywhere you go. This entails dressing suitably, being cordial and polite to locals, and refraining from actions that might be interpreted as disrespectful or objectionable.

A wonderful time!Finally, it's critical to keep in mind that traveling is all about having fun and experiencing new things. While it's crucial to act responsibly and with respect, don't forget to unwind, take in Bruges' sights and sounds, and have fun.

Bruges is a city that provides tourists with a plethora of chances to discover, acquaint themselves with, and engage with the rich culture and history of this special location. Tourists can guarantee a successful and delightful journey that they will remember for years by adhering to these additional guidelines.

## Recommendations

Visitors from all over the world can enjoy an exceptional and unforgettable vacation experience in Bruges. There is plenty for everyone to enjoy in this magnificent city, from the stunning architecture and historical landmarks to the delectable cuisine and welcoming residents. We've covered a lot of topics in our travel guide that travelers to Bruges should think about, such as safety and security, money and tipping, language and customs, and further advice for a good trip.

Along with these things to think about, there are a few tips that can help visitors get the most out of their time in Bruges. These suggestions consist of:

Bruges is frequently referred to as the "Venice of the North" due of its large network of canals. Explore the canals. A wonderful way to explore the city from a different angle and take in the breathtaking landscape is to take a boat trip or rent a paddleboat.

Visit the Markt: The Markt is Bruges' central plaza and the location of the Provinciaal Hof and the Belfry tower, two significant landmarks. One of the many outdoor cafes is an excellent place to have a drink or a meal.

**Take a chocolate tour:** Bruges is no exception to Belgium's renown for chocolate. A fantastic opportunity to learn about Belgian chocolate history and taste some of the best chocolate in the world is to go on a chocolate tour.

**Visit the galleries:** Bruges is home to a number of renowned galleries, such as the Groeningemuseum and the Memling Museum. These museums are a must-see for art enthusiasts and provide a window into Bruges' extensive cultural history.

**Attend a neighborhood festival:** Bruges hosts a number of events all year long, including the renowned Christmas markets and the Procession of the Holy Blood. Experience the local customs and culture of Bruges by going to a local festival.

**Try the beer:** Bruges is home to various breweries and taverns that provide a variety of regional beers. Belgium is another country known for its beer. A terrific way to appreciate the local culture and unwind after a day of sightseeing is to try the local beer.

Visitors from all over the world can enjoy an exceptional and unforgettable vacation experience in Bruges. Tourists can guarantee a successful and delightful journey that they will remember for years by adhering to the considerations and suggestions covered in this travel guide. There is something for everyone to enjoy in this lovely city, from discovering the canals and sites to tasting the delectable cuisine and attending local events.

Made in the USA
Monee, IL
24 May 2023

34477595R00075